Sex position: Physical And Emotional Benefits Of Different sex style

Nelson George

Table of contents

Chapter 4: Special Considerations and Safety Tips

Chapter 5: Conclusion

Chapter 1

Introduction

Sex is not just a physical act, it also has emotional and psychological benefits that can improve our overall well-being. Sexual activity can help reduce stress and anxiety, improve intimacy and connection with a partner, and increase pleasure and satisfaction. In this guide, we will explore the physical and emotional benefits of different sex positions and how they can enhance our sexual experiences. We will also discuss how communication and consent are vital in any sexual encounter, and how different positions can cater to the needs of different individuals, including those with physical limitations. This guide is intended to be informative and educational and should not be used as a substitute for professional advice or medical treatment."

It's important to note that everyone's sexual preferences and needs are different, and what works for one person may not work for another. This guide is not meant to be prescriptive, but rather to provide information and inspiration for individuals to explore different positions and find what works best for them and their partner(s). Additionally, it's important to remember that consent and communication are key in any sexual encounter and should always be prioritized. The purpose of this guide is to provide information on the various positions and the possible benefits, but most importantly it's to empower individuals to make informed decisions about their sexual lives and to feel comfortable discussing and exploring their desires with their partners.

Definition of Sex Positions

A sex position is the physical configuration of two or more individuals during sexual activity. There are various sex positions, each with its own set of benefits and variations. Some positions may focus on deeper penetration, while others may focus on stimulating specific areas such as the G-spot or the clitoris. Some positions may be better suited for individuals with physical limitations, while others may be more challenging and require more flexibility. In this guide, we will explore the different sex positions and their benefits, as well as provide tips for how to make the most of each position. It's important to remember that communication and consent are key in any sexual encounter and should always be prioritized. It's also important to be open-minded and willing to explore different positions to find what works best for you and your partner(s)."

It's also important to note that sex positions are not just about physical pleasure, but also emotional and psychological pleasure as well. Some positions may be better suited for increasing intimacy and connection with a partner, while others may be better for increasing pleasure and orgasm. Additionally, some positions may be better for individuals with physical limitations, such as positions that don't require a lot of flexibility or that can be modified to accommodate those limitations. The key is to be open-minded and willing to explore different positions to find what works best for you and your partner(s) and to always prioritize communication and consent. Remember that there is no one "right" way to have sex and that every individual and couple is unique and should feel free to explore and discover what works best for them.

Purpose of the Guide

The purpose of this guide is to provide information and inspiration on the various sex positions and to explore the physical and emotional benefits of different positions. This guide aims to educate individuals on how different positions can enhance their sexual experiences and cater to their specific needs and preferences. It also aims to empower individuals to make informed decisions about their sexual lives and to feel comfortable discussing and exploring their desires with their partners.

This guide is intended to be informative and educational and should not be used as a substitute for professional advice or medical treatment. It's important to remember that everyone's sexual preferences and needs are different, and what works for one person may not work for another. Therefore, this guide should be used as a starting point for individuals to explore and discover what works best for them and their partner(s). Communication and consent are key in any sexual encounter and should always be prioritized. The guide is not prescriptive, but rather provides information and inspiration for individuals to explore different positions and find what works best for them. "

It is also important to note that the guide is not limited to individuals who are in a traditional romantic relationship, but also inclusive of people in any kind of consensual relationship, including solo sexual activities. The guide encourages the readers to be open-minded, and creative and to prioritize their pleasure and well-being.

It is also important to understand that sex positions are not just about physical pleasure, but also emotional and psychological pleasure as well. Different positions can have different effects on emotions and intimacy, and it is important to keep this in mind when choosing a position. The guide encourages readers to take time to explore different positions, communicate with their partners, and discover what works best for them.

In summary, the purpose of the guide is to provide information, and inspiration and empower individuals to make informed decisions about their sexual lives, to feel comfortable discussing and exploring their desires with their partners, to prioritize their pleasure and well-being, and to be open-minded, creative, and inclusive.

Chapter 2

Physical Benefits of Different Sex Positions

Missionary Position

The missionary position, also known as the man-on-top position, is a classic and popular sexual position that offers a variety of physical benefits for both partners. One of the main physical benefits of the missionary position is that it allows for deep penetration, which can lead to more intense orgasms for both partners. This is because the man can fully enter the woman, allowing for greater stimulation of the G-spot and other sensitive areas.

Another physical benefit of the missionary position is that it allows for greater control over the pace and depth of penetration. This is because the man is on top and able to control the movement and thrusting, which can be beneficial for both partners.

Additionally, the missionary position can also help to improve the man's stamina and endurance, as it requires him to use his core and leg muscles to maintain the position. This can also help to improve the man's sexual stamina, allowing him to last longer during intercourse.

The missionary position can also help to improve communication and intimacy between partners, as it allows for face-to-face contact and the ability to look into each other's eyes during intercourse. The missionary position is a versatile and physically beneficial sexual position that can lead to deeper penetration, greater control, improved stamina, and increased intimacy between partners.

Another benefit of the missionary position is that it can help to improve flexibility and strength in the pelvic and core muscles. The woman is required to keep her legs open and flexed, which can help to improve the flexibility and strength of her pelvic floor muscles. This can also help to improve her sexual pleasure and orgasmic potential, as well as help prevent incontinence.

Additionally, the position can also help to improve blood flow and circulation to the pelvic area, which can help to increase sexual arousal and desire. This is because the position allows for increased pressure and stimulation of the genitals, which can lead to increased blood flow and arousal.

The missionary position also helps to tone the abdominal muscles of the man as he needs to hold himself and support his body weight during intercourse. The position offers a variety of physical benefits for both partners, including deep penetration, greater control, improved stamina, increased intimacy, and improved flexibility, strength, and blood flow to the pelvic area. It is a great way to achieve maximum physical pleasure while having sexual intercourse.

Doggy Style

Doggy style is a popular sexual position that has been around for centuries. This position is known for its intense pleasure and the physical benefits it can provide. In this article, we will explore the various physical benefits of doggy style and how it can improve your sexual experience.

Improved Stamina and Endurance
Doggy style is a position that requires a lot of physical exertion. The person on top has to use their upper body strength to hold themselves up while the person on the bottom is supporting their weight on their hands and knees. This position can help

improve your stamina and endurance by building up your core and upper body strength. As you become stronger and more physically fit, you will be able to last longer in this position and enjoy more intense orgasms.

Increased Flexibility

Doggy style is a position that requires a lot of flexibility. The person on top has to bend over and the person on the bottom has to arch their back. This position can help increase your flexibility by stretching your muscles and joints. As you become more flexible, you will be able to try new positions and enjoy deeper penetration.

Increased Blood Flow

Doggy style is a position that can increase blood flow to your pelvic region. This increased blood flow can help improve your sexual experience by making your genitals more sensitive and responsive to touch. This increased blood flow can also help improve your overall health by reducing your risk of heart disease and other health conditions.

Increased Intensity
Doggy style is a position that can provide intense pleasure. The deep penetration and the ability to control the speed and angle of penetration can make this position one of the most pleasurable. The intensity of this position can be increased by using sex toys such as vibrators or dildos for added stimulation.

Increased Confidence
Doggy style is a position that can help increase your sexual confidence. The ability to control the speed and angle of penetration can make you feel more in control of your body and your pleasure. This increased confidence can also help improve your relationships by making you more comfortable and confident in your sexual interactions.

Improved Core Strength

Doggy style is a position that requires a lot of core strength. The person on top has to use their abs and back muscles to hold themselves up, while the person on the bottom is supporting their weight on their hands and knees. This position can help improve your core strength by working your abs and back muscles. As you become stronger in these areas, you will be able to last longer in this position and enjoy more intense orgasms.

Improved Sexual Communication

Doggy style is a position that allows for open communication between partners. The person on top can easily talk to their partner and ask for what they want, while the person on the bottom can easily communicate their needs and desires. This open communication can help improve your sexual experience by making sure that both partners are satisfied and getting the pleasure they want.

Improved Prostate Health
For men, doggy style can help improve prostate health. This position allows for deep penetration, which can stimulate the prostate and improve blood flow to the area. This can help prevent prostate cancer and other prostate-related health issues. It is important to note that prostate health should always be a concern, and if you have any concerns, you should consult with a healthcare professional.

Increased G-spot Stimulation
Doggy style is a position that can provide intense G-spot stimulation. The deep penetration and the ability to control the angle of penetration can make this position one of the most pleasurable for women. This increased G-spot stimulation can lead to more intense orgasms and overall sexual satisfaction.

Increased Sense of Intimacy

Doggy style is a position that can provide a sense of intimacy between partners. The physical closeness and the ability to talk and communicate during the act can make this position feel more intimate and personal. This increased sense of intimacy can help improve your overall sexual experience and strengthen your relationship.

Doggy style is a position that offers a variety of physical benefits. It can help improve your stamina and endurance, increase your flexibility, increase blood flow, and provide intense pleasure. It also helps in improving core strength, sexual communication, prostate health, G-spot stimulation, and intimacy. As always, it is important to communicate with your partner and make sure that this position is comfortable and enjoyable for both of you. If you are experiencing any pain or discomfort, it is important to stop and communicate with your partner about what you need and what you are comfortable with. Remember, the most important thing is to have fun and enjoy the experience with your partner.

Cowgirl/Reverse Cowgirl

The cowgirl and reverse cowgirl positions are popular among many couples because of their versatility and the ability to achieve different types of pleasure. Both positions involve the female partner on top, facing towards or away from the male partner.

Physical Benefits:
The cowgirl and reverse cowgirl positions provide a great workout for the female partner as they use their core, legs, and arms to control the rhythm and movement. This can help to tone and strengthen the muscles in these areas. The position also allows for deeper penetration, which can be particularly pleasurable for the male partner. Additionally, the female partner can control the speed and angle of

penetration, making it easy to find the perfect spot for maximum pleasure.

Emotional Benefits:
One of the main emotional benefits of the cowgirl and reverse cowgirl positions is the sense of empowerment and control that the female partner feels. Being on top allows the female partner to take charge of the sexual experience and dictate the pace and intensity of the activity. This can be particularly liberating for women who may feel they don't have enough control in other areas of their lives.

The cowgirl and reverse cowgirl positions also allow for a great deal of intimacy and connection. The female partner can look into the eyes of the male partner, making it easy to maintain eye contact and deepen the emotional connection. Additionally, the proximity of the partners' bodies can make it easy for them to touch and caress each other, further enhancing the emotional bond.

The reverse cowgirl position allows for a different type of intimacy, as the female partner's back is facing the male partner, this allows for different types of touch and sensation, and it can bring a new level of pleasure for the couple.

It's important to note that the cowgirl and reverse cowgirl positions may not be suitable for everyone, particularly for those with certain physical limitations. If this is the case, it's important to communicate with your partner and find alternative positions that work for both of you. Additionally, it's important to be mindful of any discomfort or pain that may be felt by either partner during the position and to adjust accordingly.

It's also important to note that the cowgirl and reverse cowgirl positions can be modified to cater to different preferences and needs. For example, the female partner can lean forward or backward to change the angle of penetration, or use a pillow to prop herself up for more support. This can help to make the position more comfortable and to increase pleasure for both partners.

The cowgirl and reverse cowgirl positions are great options for couples looking to experience a wide range of pleasure and intimacy, but it's important to keep in mind that communication, consent, and comfort are always the key factors to consider when experimenting with any new position. Be open-minded, and creative, and communicate with your partner to find what works best for both of you.

Spooning

Spooning is a popular and intimate sex position where one partner (the "big spoon") lies behind the other (the "little spoon") and the two partners are facing the same direction. This position is known for its comfort and intimacy, making it a popular choice for couples who want to cuddle and connect while also engaging in sexual activity.

From a physical perspective, spooning is a great position for individuals with physical limitations as it doesn't require a lot of flexibility or strength. It's also a great option for pregnant individuals as it allows for more control over the depth of penetration and can alleviate pressure on the stomach.

From an emotional perspective, spooning is a great position for building intimacy and connection with a partner. The proximity and the feeling of being enveloped by the partner's body can create a sense of safety and security, which can lead to greater emotional bonding. Spooning also allows for easy communication and can facilitate a deeper level of trust and vulnerability between partners.

Spooning can also be a great position for couples who are looking to have a more relaxed and leisurely sexual experience. It's a great option for individuals who want to take their time and enjoy the physical sensations of sex without feeling the pressure to perform.

In addition, spooning is a great position for couples to engage in synchronized breathing which can enhance the pleasure and intimacy of the experience. Synchronized breathing can also help to release tension and stress, and can promote feelings of relaxation and well-being.

It's important to remember that communication and consent are key in any sexual encounter and should always be prioritized. Spooning is a position that can be tailored to the individual's specific needs and preferences. For example, couples can experiment with different angles of penetration, and with using pillows and other props for added comfort.

It's also worth mentioning that spooning can be a great position for couples of all genders and orientations. It can be adapted for vaginal, anal, or oral sex and can be a great option for couples who are looking for a position that allows for deep penetration. Also, it's a great position for couples who want to engage in anal sex, as the big spoon can provide support and stability for the little spoon.

Another benefit of spooning is that it can be a great option for couples who are looking for a position that allows for easy access to the clitoris or the prostate. The big spoon can easily reach around and stimulate these sensitive areas, which can greatly enhance the pleasure of the experience.

In conclusion, spooning is a sex position that offers a wide range of physical and emotional benefits. Its comfort and intimacy make it a great option for couples looking to cuddle and connect, while its relaxed nature makes it a great option for couples looking for a more leisurely sexual experience. It can be a great option for individuals with physical limitations, pregnant individuals, and couples of all genders and orientations. With its versatility and easy adaptability, spooning is a position that is worth exploring and experimenting with.

Standing Position

Standing positions offer a unique physical and emotional experience during sexual activity. The standing position allows for deeper penetration and can be a great option for individuals who are looking for a more intense and passionate experience. It also allows for a greater range of motion and can be a great option for individuals who have trouble achieving orgasm in other positions.

One of the main physical benefits of the standing position is that it allows for deeper penetration. This can be particularly beneficial for individuals with a penis, as it allows them to reach deeper areas of the vagina or anus. Additionally, the standing position can also be a great option for individuals who have trouble achieving orgasm in other positions, as the deeper penetration can help increase stimulation and pleasure.

The standing position also allows for a greater range of motion, which can make it a great option for individuals who enjoy experimenting with different angles and positions. This can make it a great option for individuals who are looking for a more dynamic and exciting sexual experience.

On an emotional level, the standing position can also be a great option for individuals who are looking to add some passion and intensity to their sexual encounters. The position allows for more intimate and face-to-face contact, which can help increase emotional connection and intimacy. Additionally, standing positions can also help individuals feel more in control and dominant, which can be particularly beneficial for individuals who may feel more submissive in other positions.

It's important to note that the standing position can also be a bit more challenging physically, as it may require more balance and strength. Additionally, individuals with physical limitations or mobility issues may have difficulty with this position. In such cases, it's important to communicate with your partner and explore modifications or alternative positions that work for both of you.

Couples who are looking to add some spontaneity and excitement to their sexual encounters. The standing position can be used in various places such as in the kitchen, against a wall, or even in a shower. This can add an element of surprise and adventure to sexual encounters and can help reignite passion and excitement in a relationship.

Another benefit of the standing position is that it can be a great option for individuals who are looking for a more challenging and physically demanding sexual experience. The position can help increase cardiovascular health and provide a great workout for both partners.

The standing position can also be a great option for individuals who want to try different angles and positions. For example, a woman can bend over and the man can penetrate from behind, this can increase the stimulation of her G-spot and provide a new and exciting experience.

It's also important to note that the standing position can be modified to cater to the needs of different individuals. For example, individuals who have difficulty standing for long periods can use a wall or a chair for support. Additionally, individuals who have difficulty balancing can use a bed or a couch to help support themselves.

In conclusion, the standing position offers a unique physical and emotional experience during sexual activity. It allows for deeper penetration, and a greater range of motion, and can be a great option for individuals who are looking for a more intense, passionate, and exciting experience. Additionally, it can be a great option for couples who are looking to add some spontaneity and excitement to their sexual encounters and can be modified to cater to the needs of different individuals. It's important to be open-minded and willing to explore different positions to find what works best for you and your partner(s) and to always prioritize communication and consent.

Chapter 3

Emotional Benefits of Different Sex Positions

Intimacy and Bonding

Intimacy and bonding are crucial components of any sexual encounter, and they can have a profound impact on our emotional well-being. Intimacy is the emotional and psychological connection between two individuals, and it can be achieved through various forms of physical and emotional contact. Bonding, on the other hand, is the emotional and psychological connection that is created through shared experiences and mutual trust and understanding.

One of the main emotional benefits of intimacy and bonding is that they can help reduce stress and anxiety. Studies have shown that individuals who have a strong emotional connection with their partners have lower levels of stress and anxiety and are better able to cope with life's challenges. Additionally, intimacy and bonding can also help individuals feel more secure and supported, which can be particularly beneficial for individuals who may feel lonely or isolated.

Intimacy and bonding can also help increase pleasure and satisfaction during sexual activity. When individuals feel emotionally connected to their partners, they are more likely to feel comfortable and relaxed during sexual activity, which can help increase pleasure and satisfaction. Additionally, individuals who feel emotionally connected to their partners are also more likely to feel comfortable exploring their desires and experimenting with different positions and techniques, which can help increase pleasure and satisfaction.

Another benefit of intimacy and bonding is that it can help increase emotional connection and intimacy. When individuals feel emotionally connected to their partners, they are more likely to open up and share their thoughts, feelings, and desires. This can help create a deeper level of understanding and connection between partners, which can help improve communication and intimacy.

Intimacy and bonding can also help improve overall relationship satisfaction. Studies have shown that individuals who have a strong emotional connection with their partners are more likely to be satisfied with their relationships and report a higher level of overall happiness.

In addition to the emotional benefits, intimacy and bonding can also have a positive impact on physical health. Studies have shown that individuals who have a strong emotional connection with their partners have a stronger immune system, lower blood pressure, and a lower risk of heart disease. This is because intimacy and bonding can help reduce stress and promote feelings of safety and security, which can have a positive impact on overall physical health.

Another important aspect of intimacy and bonding is that it can help foster feelings of self-worth and self-acceptance. When individuals feel emotionally connected to their partners and can openly communicate and express their desires, they are more likely to feel accepted and valued for who they are. This can help improve self-esteem and self-confidence, which can have a positive impact on overall emotional well-being.

It's also important to note that intimacy and bonding are not limited to sexual activity, but can be achieved through various forms of physical and emotional contact. Holding hands, cuddling, kissing, and even talking and listening can all help create a deeper level of emotional connection and intimacy.

Intimacy and bonding can help reduce stress and anxiety, increase pleasure and satisfaction, increase emotional connection and intimacy, improve overall relationship satisfaction, and foster feelings of self-worth and self-acceptance. It's important to prioritize communication and consent and to be open-minded and willing to explore different ways of creating intimacy and bonding with your partner(s).

Improved Communication

Communication is a key aspect of any sexual encounter, and it is essential for individuals to feel comfortable discussing and exploring their desires with their partners. Improved communication can lead to a variety of emotional benefits, including increased trust, intimacy, and pleasure.

One of the main emotional benefits of improved communication is increased trust. When individuals can openly and honestly communicate their desires and boundaries with their partners, it can help build trust and understanding in the relationship. This can lead to a more fulfilling and satisfying sexual experience for both partners.

Another emotional benefit of improved communication is increased intimacy. When individuals can communicate openly and honestly about their desires, it can help increase emotional connection and intimacy. Being able to discuss and explore different fantasies and desires with a partner can help create a deeper emotional bond and can lead to a more satisfying sexual experience.

Improved communication can also lead to increased pleasure. When individuals can communicate openly and honestly about their desires, it can help ensure that both partners are on the same page and can fully enjoy the sexual experience. This can lead to a more satisfying and fulfilling sexual experience for both partners.

Another emotional benefit of improved communication is that it can help individuals feel more confident and secure in their sexual experiences. When individuals can communicate openly and honestly about their desires and boundaries, it can help them feel more comfortable and confident in their sexual encounters. This can lead to a more enjoyable and satisfying sexual experience for both partners.

It can also help to decrease the chances of misunderstandings and conflicts. When individuals can communicate openly and honestly about their desires and boundaries, it can help to prevent misunderstandings and conflicts from arising in the relationship. This can lead to a more peaceful and harmonious relationship.

It's important to note that communication is not just about talking, it also includes active listening, being attentive and responsive to your partner's needs, and understanding that everyone's desires, boundaries, and preferences are different. It's also important to remember that communication is a continuous process, and it's important to check in with your partner regularly to ensure that everyone's needs are being met.

Improved communication is essential for a fulfilling and satisfying sexual experience. It leads to increased trust, intimacy, pleasure, confidence, and satisfaction. It helps individuals to feel comfortable discussing and exploring their desires with their partners, and it can help ensure that both partners are on the same page and able to fully enjoy the sexual experience. It also helps to prevent misunderstandings and conflicts. It's important to remember that communication is a continuous process and it's important to check in with your partner regularly to ensure that everyone's needs are being met.

Increased Confidence and Self-Esteem

Sexual activity can have a profound impact on our emotional well-being, particularly when it comes to confidence and self-esteem. Engaging in sexual activity can help individuals feel more confident in their bodies and their sexual abilities, which can lead to increased self-esteem and a greater sense of self-worth.

One of the main emotional benefits of sexual activity is that it can help individuals feel more confident in their bodies. This can be particularly beneficial for individuals who may have body image issues or feel self-conscious about their bodies. Engaging in sexual activity can help individuals feel more comfortable and confident in their bodies, which can lead to increased self-esteem and a greater sense of self-worth.

Additionally, sexual activity can also help individuals feel more confident in their sexual abilities. This can be particularly beneficial for individuals who may have sexual performance anxiety or feel self-conscious about their sexual abilities. Engaging in sexual activity can help individuals feel more comfortable and confident in their sexual abilities, which can lead to increased self-esteem and a greater sense of self-worth.

Sexual activity can also help individuals feel more connected to their partners, which can lead to increased self-esteem and a greater sense of self-worth. Engaging in sexual activity can help individuals feel more connected to their partners emotionally and physically, which can lead to increased self-esteem and a greater sense of self-worth.

It's important to note that increased confidence and self-esteem are not always immediate results of sexual activity, but rather a gradual process that comes with time and practice. It's also important to note that sexual activity should always be consensual and that communication and consent are key in any sexual encounter.

It's also important to note that increased confidence and self-esteem can also come from exploring and experimenting with different sexual positions, as well as communication and consent. Exploring different positions and techniques can help individuals feel more comfortable and confident in their sexual abilities, which can lead to increased self-esteem and a greater sense of self-worth. Additionally, communication and consent can help individuals feel more comfortable and confident in their sexual abilities, as they can express their desires and boundaries freely and openly.

It's important to remember that sexual activity should always be consensual and that communication and consent are key in any sexual encounter. Individuals who feel pressured or coerced into sexual activity may experience negative emotional consequences, such as decreased self-esteem and confidence.

In addition, sexual activity can also provide an emotional release and help individuals deal with stress and anxiety. This can lead to improved mental well-being, which in turn can positively impact confidence and self-esteem.

It's also important to note that sexual health and sexual education are important for increasing confidence and self-esteem. Understanding our bodies and how they function, as well as learning about different sexual positions, techniques and communication can help individuals feel more confident and secure in their sexual encounters.

Sexual activity can have a positive impact on emotional well-being, particularly when it comes to confidence and self-esteem. It can help individuals feel more confident in their bodies and sexual abilities, as well as provide emotional release and stress relief. Communication, consent, and sexual education are key in any sexual encounter, and it's important to remember that increased confidence and self-esteem are not immediate results but rather a gradual process that comes with time and practice.

Stress Relief

Sexual activity has been shown to have several emotional benefits, one of which is stress relief. Stress is a normal part of life, but when it becomes chronic, it can hurt our physical and emotional well-being. Sexual activity can be an effective way to reduce stress and improve overall well-being.

One of the main emotional benefits of sexual activity is that it can help reduce stress. During sexual activity, the body releases several hormones, including oxytocin and endorphins. Oxytocin, also known as the "cuddle hormone", is responsible for promoting feelings of bonding and attachment, while endorphins are responsible for reducing pain and promoting feelings of pleasure and euphoria. Together, these hormones can help reduce stress and promote feelings of relaxation and well-being.

Additionally, sexual activity can also help reduce feelings of anxiety. Anxiety is a normal stress response, but when it becomes chronic, it can harm our emotional well-being. Sexual activity can help reduce anxiety by promoting feelings of pleasure and relaxation, which can help distract individuals from their worries and concerns.

Another benefit of sexual activity is that it can help improve communication and emotional intimacy with a partner. Stress can put a strain on relationships, but engaging in sexual activity with a partner can help improve communication and emotional intimacy, which can help strengthen the relationship and reduce stress.

It's important to note that sexual activity may not be the best stress relief option for everyone, and it's important to consider individual preferences and comfort levels. Additionally, it's important to remember that sexual activity should always be consensual and that communication and consent are key in any sexual encounter.

It's also important to note that sexual activity can be a great form of self-care and self-compassion. Stress can lead to feelings of self-doubt, guilt, and shame, however, engaging in consensual sexual activity can be a way of taking care of oneself, and promoting self-acceptance, self-compassion and self-appreciation. Sexual activity can also be a form of mindfulness, allowing individuals to focus on the present moment, and to release negative thoughts and emotions. This can help reduce stress and promote feelings of peace and tranquility.

Moreover, sexual activity can also be a way to improve one's sleep, as the release of endorphins and oxytocin can help promote feelings of relaxation, which can lead to better and more restful sleep. Stress can cause insomnia and a lack of sleep, but sexual activity can help reduce the negative impact of stress on sleep.

It's also essential to mention that sexual activity can be a form of release, as stress and anxiety can build up over time, and sexual activity can provide a way to release that tension and pressure. This can help individuals feel more in control of their emotions and promote feelings of empowerment.

Overall, sexual activity can provide several emotional benefits, including stress relief, improved communication and emotional intimacy with a partner, self-care, mindfulness, better sleep, and release of tension. It's important to consider individual preferences and comfort levels and to always prioritize communication and consent. It's essential to remember that sexual activity should be consensual, and it should be a way to promote positive emotions, self-compassion, and self-care, not a way of dealing with stress or pressure.

Chapter 4

Special Considerations and Safety Tips

Sexual activity should always be consensual and safe for all parties involved. It's important to consider any special considerations or safety precautions that may be necessary to ensure that the experience is enjoyable and comfortable for everyone.

One important special consideration is the use of protection. It's important to protect against unwanted pregnancies and sexually transmitted infections (STIs) by using appropriate forms of contraception and practicing safe sex. This includes using condoms, dental dams, or other forms of barrier protection. It's also essential to discuss STI testing and vaccination with your partner(s) and to stay informed about the risks and best practices for preventing STIs.

Another special consideration is individual physical limitations or disabilities. It's important to communicate with your partner(s) about any physical limitations or disabilities and to explore different positions or modifications that may make the experience more comfortable and enjoyable for everyone involved.

It's also important to consider any mental or emotional limitations or conditions that may impact sexual activity. This can include issues such as anxiety or trauma, and it's important to communicate with your partner(s) and to seek professional help if necessary.

It's also important to consider any cultural or religious considerations that may impact sexual activity. This includes respecting any cultural or religious beliefs that may affect sexual behavior and always seeking consent from all parties involved.

It's important to have open and honest communication with your partner(s) about any boundaries or limits and to respect these boundaries at all times. This includes verbal and non-verbal cues, and it's important to stop any activity if one of the parties is uncomfortable or wants to stop.

Another special consideration is the impact of certain medications or medical conditions on sexual activity. Some medications may affect sexual function or desire, while certain medical conditions may make certain positions or activities uncomfortable or even dangerous. It's important to discuss any such considerations with your partner(s) and healthcare provider and to explore alternative positions or activities that may be more comfortable or safe.

It's also important to consider the impact of alcohol and drugs on sexual activity. The use of alcohol or drugs can impair judgment and increase the risk of unwanted or unsafe sexual activity. It's important to make informed and conscious decisions about sexual activity while under the influence and to prioritize communication and consent at all times.

It's also important to consider the location and privacy when engaging in sexual activity. It's important to ensure that all parties involved are comfortable with the location and that the activity is taking place in a private and safe space. It's important to remember that sexual activity should be a positive and enjoyable experience for all parties involved. By considering special considerations and safety precautions, communication and consent, keeping an open mind, and being respectful of everyone's boundaries and comfort levels, sexual activity can be a positive and fulfilling experience for all parties.

Pregnancy and Medical Conditions

During pregnancy, it's important to consult with your healthcare provider to determine what positions and activities are safe and appropriate. Some positions may be uncomfortable or even dangerous during certain stages of pregnancy, and it's important to listen to your body and avoid any positions or activities that cause pain or discomfort. Additionally, it's important to discuss any concerns or questions you may have with your healthcare provider.

Certain medical conditions can also impact sexual activity, and it's important to consult with your healthcare provider to determine what positions and activities are safe and appropriate. For example, individuals with back or knee problems may find it more comfortable to engage in sexual activity in positions that put less stress on these areas. Additionally, individuals with certain medical conditions, such as heart disease or diabetes, may need to take extra precautions to ensure that sexual activity is safe for them.

It's also important to consider the use of medication and how it may affect sexual activity. Some medications may affect sexual function or desire or may cause other side effects that may impact sexual activity. It's important to discuss any concerns or questions you may have with your healthcare provider.

Additionally, it's important to remember that communication and consent are key in any sexual encounter, and it's important to discuss any concerns or limitations with your partner(s) and to respect their boundaries and comfort levels.

It's important to note that certain medical conditions and pregnancy may require modification of sexual positions and activities, but it doesn't mean that sexual activity should be stopped. With the guidance of a healthcare provider, it's possible to adapt and find new ways to enjoy a sexual activity that are safe and comfortable for everyone involved. It's important to be open-minded and willing to explore different positions and activities and to always prioritize communication and consent.

It's also important to remember that sexual activity during pregnancy and with certain medical conditions may not be the same as it was before and it's important to accept that and find new ways to enjoy a sexual activity that is safe and comfortable for everyone involved.

Sexual activity during pregnancy and with certain medical conditions can be a bit more complicated, but it's important to consult with a healthcare provider to determine what positions and activities are safe and appropriate. It's also important to consider the use of medication and how it may affect the sexual activity and to communicate and seek consent from all parties involved. With the guidance of a healthcare provider, it's possible to adapt and find new ways to enjoy a sexual activity that are safe and comfortable for everyone involved, and it's important to always prioritize communication, and consent, and respect boundaries and comfort levels.

Consent and Communication

Consent and communication are essential components of safe and enjoyable sexual activity. They involve actively seeking and giving permission, discussing boundaries and desires, and respecting the choices and comfort levels of all parties involved.

Consent is the act of willingly agreeing to engage in sexual activity. It's important to remember that consent must be given freely and enthusiastically and that it can be withdrawn at any time. It's also important to remember that consent must be given for each act or activity, and that past consent does not automatically imply future consent.

Communication is the act of discussing boundaries, desires, and concerns with your partner(s). It's important to have open and honest communication about sexual activity and to discuss any limitations or concerns that may arise. This includes discussing any physical or emotional limitations, discussing any medical conditions or pregnancy, and discussing any cultural or religious considerations.

It's important to remember that communication and consent are ongoing processes and that they should be continuously sought and given throughout any sexual encounter. It's also important to remember that communication and consent are not just about saying yes or no, but also about discussing and respecting boundaries, desires, and comfort levels.

It's important to remember that consent and communication are not only important for preventing unwanted or unsafe sexual activity, but also for ensuring that the experience is enjoyable and fulfilling for all parties involved.

It's also important to remember that consent and communication are not only important for couples, but also any kind of consensual sexual activity, including solo sexual activities. It's important to respect one's boundaries and desires and to communicate them effectively to oneself.

It's also important to note that consent and communication can be challenging at times, and it's important to be patient and understanding with yourself and your partner(s). It may take time to develop effective communication and consent practices, and it's important to be willing to learn and grow as individuals and as partners.

It's also important to remember that consent and communication can be affected by societal and cultural influences, and it's important to be aware of and challenge any harmful beliefs or attitudes that may impact sexual activity. This includes challenging ideas related to gender, sexuality, and power dynamics, and actively working to create a culture of consent and communication.

It's also important to remember that consent and communication can be affected by power imbalances and it's important to be aware of and address any power imbalances that may impact sexual activity. This includes being aware of and addressing issues related to age, status, and physical or mental capacity, and actively working to create a culture of mutual respect and understanding.

Consent and communication are essential elements of safe and enjoyable sexual activity. They involve actively seeking and giving permission, discussing boundaries and desires, and respecting the choices and comfort levels of all parties involved. It's important to remember that consent and communication can be challenging at times, and it's important to be patient and understanding with yourself and your partner(s). It's also important to be aware of and challenge any societal or cultural influences that may impact sexual activity and to be aware of and address any power imbalances that may impact sexual activity. Prioritizing consent and communication can help ensure that sexual activity is safe, enjoyable, and fulfilling for all parties involved.

Lubrication and Comfort

Lubrication and comfort are essential components of safe and enjoyable sexual activity. Lubrication helps to reduce friction and discomfort during sexual activity, while comfort involves ensuring that the physical and emotional needs of all parties involved are met.

Lubrication is a natural or synthetic substance that is used to reduce friction and discomfort during sexual activity. It's important to use enough lubrication to ensure that sexual activity is comfortable for all parties involved. Lubrication is especially important for individuals who experience vaginal dryness or for those engaging in anal sex. It's important to note that saliva, lotion, and cooking oil should not be used as a lubricant as they can cause irritation or infection.

Comfort is the physical and emotional well-being of all parties involved during sexual activity. It involves ensuring that the physical needs, such as position, lighting, and temperature, are met, as well as emotional needs, such as trust, safety, and communication. It's important to remember that comfort levels can vary from person to person, and it's important to communicate and respect the boundaries and comfort levels of all parties involved.

It's important to remember that lubrication and comfort are not only important for vaginal and anal sex, but also any kind of sexual activity, including oral sex and masturbation. It's important to ensure that enough lubrication is used and to ensure that the physical and emotional needs of all parties involved are met.

It's also important to note that lubrication and comfort can be affected by certain medical conditions or medication, and it's important to consult with a healthcare provider to determine what lubricants or comfort measures may be appropriate. It's also important to communicate with your partner(s) about any concerns or limitations related to lubrication and comfort and to respect their boundaries and comfort levels. It's also important to be aware of any allergies or sensitivities when it comes to lubricants and to choose a lubricant that suits everyone's needs and comfort.

In conclusion, lubrication and comfort are essential components of safe and enjoyable sexual activity. Lubrication helps to reduce friction and discomfort during sexual activity, while comfort involves ensuring that the physical and emotional needs of all parties involved are met. It's important to use enough lubrication to ensure that sexual activity is comfortable for all parties involved and to communicate and respect the boundaries and comfort levels of all parties involved. Lubrication and comfort are not only important for vaginal and anal sex, but also any kind of sexual activity, including oral sex and masturbation. It's important to be aware of any allergies or sensitivities when it comes to lubricants and to choose a lubricant that suits everyone's needs and comfort. It's also important to be aware of any medical conditions or medication that may impact lubrication and comfort and to consult with a healthcare provider to determine what lubricants or comfort measures may be appropriate.

Chapter 5

Conclusion

In conclusion, sexual activity can be a positive and fulfilling experience when it's consensual, safe, and comfortable for all parties involved. By exploring different positions, techniques, and considerations, individuals can expand their understanding of intimacy and pleasure.

In this guide, we've explored various topics related to sexual activity, including:

Definition of sex positions
Physical and emotional benefits of different positions
Special considerations and safety tips
Pregnancy and medical conditions
Consent and communication
Lubrication and comfort

Each of these topics is crucial in understanding how to make sexual activity more enjoyable and safe. We've highlighted the importance of communication, consent, and respect for boundaries and comfort levels.

It's important to remember that sexual activity should be consensual and safe for all parties involved. It's important to consider any special considerations or safety precautions, such as the use of protection, physical limitations, mental or emotional conditions, cultural or religious considerations, and open and honest communication about boundaries and limits.

It's also important to remember that sexual activity during pregnancy and with certain medical conditions may require modification of sexual positions and activities, but it doesn't mean that sexual activity should be stopped. With the guidance of a healthcare provider, it's possible to adapt and find new ways to enjoy a sexual activity that are safe and comfortable for everyone involved.

Lubrication and comfort are also key elements of safe and enjoyable sexual activity, it's important to use enough lubrication to ensure that sexual activity is comfortable for all parties involved, and to communicate and respect the boundaries and comfort levels of all parties involved.

In summary, sexual activity can be a positive and fulfilling experience when it's consensual, safe, and comfortable for all parties involved. By prioritizing communication, consent, and respect for boundaries and comfort levels, and considering special considerations and safety tips, lubrication and comfort, individuals can expand their understanding of intimacy and pleasure, and make sexual activity a positive and enjoyable experience for all parties involved."

Summary of Key Points

Sexual activity should be consensual and safe for all parties involved.

It's important to consider any special considerations or safety precautions, such as the use of protection, physical limitations, mental or emotional conditions, cultural or religious considerations, and open and honest communication about boundaries and limits.

It's important to prioritize communication, consent, and respect for boundaries and comfort levels throughout any sexual encounter.

Lubrication and comfort are essential components of safe and enjoyable sexual activity.

During pregnancy or medical conditions, it's important to consult with a healthcare provider to determine what positions and activities are safe and appropriate.

It's important to be aware of any allergies or sensitivities when it comes to lubricants and to choose a lubricant that suits everyone's needs and comfort.

Communication and consent should be ongoing processes and are also important for solo sexual activities

Sexual activity can be adapted and enjoyed even during pregnancy or medical conditions with the guidance of a healthcare provider.

Societal and cultural influences should be acknowledged and challenged to create a culture of consent and communication.

Power imbalances should be acknowledged and addressed to create mutual respect and understanding.
By following the key points, sexual activity can be a positive and fulfilling experience for all parties involved."

Additional Resources

In addition to this guide, there are many other resources available for individuals who wish to learn more about sexual activity and intimacy. These include:

Books: There are many books available on sexual activity, intimacy, and relationships. These books cover a wide range of topics, including positions, techniques, communication, and consent. Some books are written for specific populations, such as individuals with disabilities, older adults, or same-sex couples.

Websites: There are many websites available that provide information on sexual activity, intimacy, and relationships. These websites cover a wide range of topics, including positions, techniques, communication, and consent. Some websites are written for specific populations, such as individuals with disabilities, older adults, or same-sex couples.

Online communities: There are many online communities available for individuals who wish to connect with others who share their interests in sexual activity and intimacy. These communities provide a safe and supportive space for individuals to share information, ask questions, and get support from others who understand their experiences.

Healthcare Providers: Consult with a healthcare provider for any concerns or questions you may have about sexual activity, intimacy, and relationships. Healthcare providers can guide safe sexual practices, contraception options, and other related issues.

Therapy or counseling: Individuals who may have any emotional or mental challenges that may affect their sexual activity, intimacy, and relationship can seek therapy or counseling. This can help individuals work through any emotional or mental challenges they may be facing and help them build stronger and more fulfilling relationships.

It's important to remember that everyone's needs and experiences are different, and it's important to find the resources that are right for you. By exploring the available resources, individuals can expand their understanding of sexual activity and intimacy and make informed decisions about their sexual relationships.